Effective Communication

A Guide to Speaking Clearly and Positively Influencing Others

By

Zach Hersey

Table of Contents

Introduction   4

Chapter 1   9
**Reasons for the Significance of Effective
Communication**   9

Chapter 2   18
Methods of Communication   18

Chapter 3   28
Overcoming Difficulties When Speaking Publicly   28

Chapter 4   35
Expressing Empathy in Communication   35

Chapter 5   50
Creating Emotional Bonds   50

Introduction

Communication is the most crucial aspect of our life. It determines the ties made with the persons in personal and professional life.

Effective communication offers a foundation for trust and respect to flourish. It also allows us to comprehend a person better and the context of the interaction. Individuals typically assume that their communication abilities are far greater than what they are. Communication looks simple; nonetheless, most of what two people say is been misunderstood thereby leading to conflicts and suffering.

To communicate effectively one must comprehend the emotions underlying the issue being discussed. Knowing how to speak effectively may strengthen the connections one has at home, work, and in social activities.

Understanding communication skills such as listening, non-verbal communication, and controlling stress may assist in strengthening the connections one has with others.

One important factor of communication is listening. An excellent listener is one who, not only comprehends how the speaker feels but, also knows what they are communicating. Building a deep connection between the speaker and the listener is one of the first stages to becoming a good listener. To develop this connection speakers should first be in a setting with open-minded listeners which allows them to feel more comfortable to voice their thoughts, emotions, and ideas.

Listeners should refrain from becoming judgmental. A person does not have to agree with the beliefs, values, or viewpoints of what is said rather to completely comprehend them, one must set aside their criticism. Speakers feel they can trust the listeners with their knowledge when they know that they will not be judged.

As humans, we are attracted to one another and communicate with one another in several ways. There are various roles that each human performs daily, depending on the circumstances of an encounter. What every contact has in common is the requirement for clear and efficient communication.

There are various factors involved in building and sustaining enduring and real connections via communication, two of which are detecting body language clues and applying good listening skills.

Inappropriately making use of these aspects, one may witness an improvement in the quality of social interactions, as well as enhanced confidence in connecting with people in a social capacity. These perks may be significant tools in landing a job or developing enduring connections.

Chapter 1

Reasons for the Significance of Effective Communication

Those with effective communication skills have always benefited from it. The history of communication is extensive, and its customs continue to influence contemporary communication theories.

Oral communication played a major role in ancient communication in both the East and the West. Books and authors on the concepts of written communication emerged when writing gained prominence as a permanent record of communication.

Establishing a positive reputation and contributing to the success of the organization can be achieved through effective communication with external parties. A company can negotiate a lucrative sale, win back an unhappy client, generate demand for its product or service, promote collections, drive performance, and generally foster goodwill with the correct letter, proposal, report, phone contact, or personal chat.

Communication skills are the most important requirement for a promotable executive. People who struggle with writing or vocal communication too frequently end up stuck in low-paying, unfulfilling positions. Management personnel communicate, write, listen, and speak for sixty to ninety percent of their working hours.

In whatever situation you find yourself in, including the workplace, school, and home, effective communication is essential. This is because we live in a society where everyone is interrelated and dependent on one another for survival and success in both our personal and professional lives.

An organization's ability to communicate effectively is essential to its growth. It is something that facilitates the essential management tasks of organizing, motivating, directing, controlling, and planning. Effective communication, both in writing and verbally, is the cornerstone of any commercial endeavor.

Every aspect of a business is built around communication. It follows that the foundation of any organization is good communication.

The following are some advantages of having strong communication skills:

1. Motivation remains at the core of communication. Understanding how work is being done and making improvements when necessary helps the employer
2. Effective communication serves as a source of information, facilitates

decision-making, and aids in determining the best course of action.

3. Additionally, communication helps to shape people's attitudes. An informed person will always be more positive in attitude than someone who is not as educated.

4. Employees can develop diverse attitudes with the support of various communication channels, such as meetings, journals, and publications.

5. In the current business environment, no company can function alone. Communication is a tool that aids with socialization, which is very important.

6. It supports management's controlling process in addition to the other management duties.

It enables supervisors to be aware of complaints from their staff and assists employees in learning about company policies.

One of the fundamental components of management is communication. That plays a key role in boosting staff morale. People communicate with the management by giving various feedback and requests, whether verbally or nonverbally.

Being Content

You can experience the fulfillment that comes from being able to obtain anything you need or want by being able to express your needs and desires to others (because we are powerless to obtain what we are not able to ask for).

Decrease in Stress

Any interpersonal conflicts you may be experiencing can be greatly eased by effective communication. Additionally, it lessens misunderstandings in both your personal and professional lives, which may be a major cause of stress.

Establishing Closeness

In a relationship that unites two or more individuals, efficient communication fosters a feeling of intimacy and closeness between the parties involved. Deeper intimacy can only occur when there is effective communication, especially deep listening, which allows people to be honest and dependable in their partnerships.

Comprehending Others

You can learn a lot about other people's thoughts and feelings by practicing effective communication techniques, especially being able to listen intently and ask clarifying questions. This helps you address the requirements of others in your life, which gives you the ability to uplift others and may improve your reputation with those around you.

Comprehending

Being able to articulate your ideas and feelings to others through good verbal and nonverbal communication makes you feel accepted, united, and like a part of the group.

Time Conserving

Time savings can be greatly increased by communicating clearly. Knowing whether to connect with someone in person or via phone, email, or fax may save a company a great deal of money and effort, especially in a professional situation. If you have a time-sensitive conversation over the phone, for example, you can address topics that may be too complex for email or that require too much back and forth while also saving time compared to in-person meetings.

Chapter 2

Methods of Communication

People communicate every day, whether at home, at work, or in social settings. Communication is essential when establishing relationships and sharing ideas.

Communication is the process of conveying information from one person to another or a group of individuals. Every form of communication mechanism has at least one sender and one receiver. It is complex because effective communication can be influenced by a variety of factors, including our emotions, cultural background, communication medium, and location. Employers throughout the world value good communication abilities since they are difficult to find.

Methods of communication include:

- Verbal communication
- Non-verbal communication
- Written communication
- Listening
- Visual communication

Verbal Communication

Verbal communication is the use of spoken words to interact with others. This can be done in person with another person or group of people, over the phone, or via a video call such as Skype or Zoom. Face-to-face verbal communication is normally the preferred approach; however, it is not always feasible owing to time limits or people's locations. It might be informal, such as a casual conversation with a friend, or more official, such as a work meeting, interview, conference, lecture, or oral presentation.

The effectiveness of oral communication depends on the receiver's receptiveness, the pace, loudness, and pitch of the words, and the clarity of speech. Visual clues and body language are two examples of nonverbal communication that can help with verbal communication.

In commercial terms, verbal communication might include:

Telling stories - aids in the formation of common meanings among members of the organization. It can help employees grasp the organization's key values as well as how things are done.

Having Crucial Conversations - These are high-stakes communications, not routine office chats. This may be proposing a business concept or requesting a pay raise. These sorts of communication need talent, thinking, and planning.

Non-verbal Communication

Facial expressions, eye contact, hand motions, touch, posture, and total body movement are examples of nonverbal communication that assist you in understanding how others are feeling and thinking. These items frequently give reinforcement for vocal communication. Except when utilizing sign language, nonverbal communication is rarely employed in isolation from verbal communication.

Nonverbal communication also refers to how something is said. This includes vocal style, tone, pitch, and quality. This is known as paralanguage. Being an effective communicator entails evaluating your tone of voice, facial expressions, and body language in addition to the words you say.

Written Communication

A letter, email, report, or social media message are all forms of written communication. Written communication should seek to convey your message clearly and concisely. Too much-written information that is repetitious or unneeded will certainly lose the reader's attention and may not effectively convey your message. The effectiveness of written communication is determined by its style, grammar, vocabulary, and clarity. Written communication is useful when you need comprehensive instructions when someone is too far away or unable to speak with you.

Written communication in the form of emails is convenient since you don't have to wait for someone to become available or try to match your schedules. You can send the email, and they will read and react when they can. When considering written communication, keep in mind that in the digital age, your work is likely to be available for public viewing for a long time after you have written it. It is therefore critical to ensure that the spelling and punctuation are correct and that you are satisfied with the content. The ability to communicate in writing is essential in the business. This could be to coworkers, managers, or customers. The ability to communicate well in writing is essential for every successful business.

Written communication also provides evidence that a conversation took place. This could be because you are expressing concern about something, requesting feedback, or notifying someone about a work you have finished.

Listening

Active listening is one of the most crucial aspects of communication because it allows us to genuinely engage with the person who is speaking to us. If you don't listen during a conversation or a team meeting, you won't be able to interact or reply properly. It can be tough to sit and listen for long lengths of time when you are not expected to or do not have the opportunity to engage. This could occur during a lecture or training session. In these cases, some people opt to record the session if permitted.

Visual Communication

Visual communication can be accomplished using visual aids such as drawing, graphic design, illustration, color, typography, signs, and other electronic resources. Visual communication such as; graphs and charts, can supplement written communication and even replace it completely. Visual communication can be a more potent technique to convey a message than spoken and non-verbal communication.

Visual communication is considerably easier and more varied now, thanks to technological advancements. This also implies that visual communication might be a lot more imaginative.

Visual communication is all around us, whether it's on television, social media, or in advertisements. Advertisers utilize it to promote items or convey a particular message.

Note that, how you communicate relies on who you are interacting with and the objective of the communication. Different communication strategies are better suited to different situations, and you can choose the one that best conveys your message and communicates successfully.

Chapter 3

Overcoming Difficulties When Speaking Publicly

Do you have speech issues or fear of speaking in public? Well, you're not alone.

Overcoming the challenges of public speaking can be difficult, but with hard work and practice, you can become a confident and successful speaker. Many people have performance anxiety when faced with the task of standing on a podium or striking up a conversation with strangers. This fear might become so acute that it causes panic attacks. If you're like most individuals, you avoid public humiliation by avoiding public speaking entirely. That is not the correct approach to this problem since the more you avoid speaking in public, the more the problem worsens and becomes chronic and disruptive. Don't be fooled into staying in your comfort zone; instead, use these strategies to effectively conquer your speech problems:

Thorough Preparation: Most people are nervous about speaking in public because they believe they lack sufficient understanding of the subject at hand. They are concerned that someone in the audience may ask a difficult question that they are unprepared to answer. You may solve this difficulty by properly preparing and having confidence in your abilities to provide an optimum presentation on the topic. Make sure you rehearse and conduct extensive research. Time your rehearsal presentations to ensure that they fit into your allotted stage time.

Another way to enhance your confidence is to avoid just memorizing words. Understand every subject in the presentation so that you do not get lost throughout your speech. Memorizing word for word is dangerous since you may forget certain words or, in extreme circumstances, something may interrupt your path of thought and disturb your flow. Just remember the main ideas and subtopics, and fill in the remainder during the presentation.

Be Calm and Don't Rush: Rushing, in its most basic form, refers to speaking quickly without regard for whether your views are obvious or not, or without regard for your body language. When you speak quickly, your breathing patterns shift, and you get shortness and shallowness of breath. You may occasionally run short of air or be compelled to stop breathing abruptly. This is not a good indicator since others will sense your restlessness and begin to analyze you as a person rather than focusing on what you have to say. If you lose touch with your audience, they appear unpleasant, which raises your tension.

Practicing Voice Control: If you want to practice voice control, you may use a variety of various speech plans. At the end of the exercise, you will learn how to breathe via the diaphragm rather than the chest. Diaphragmatic breathing is an essential tool for all public performers, including singers, clergy, and public speeches. It enables you to hold notes and speak for extended periods without running out of breath. You will sound fantastic throughout the presentation, regardless of length.

Engaging the Audience in a Conversation: The idea is to make your presentation a two-way conversation rather than a monologue. The issue of delivering a monologue is that you will be responsible for both informing and entertaining the audience. Unless you are a comic, eliminating audience boredom during a monologue is nearly difficult. Two-way interaction, on the other hand, enables you to ask questions and engage the audience to keep them interested. Giving them a minute to argue between themselves helps you to take a break and regroup your ideas.

Body Language: Your body language reveals almost as much information as what you say, if not more. Do not let your nervousness show in your facial expressions or standing position. Be mindful of your hand placement, standing stance, facial emotions, and stage movements.

Stage presence is key: Be present and demonstrate sufficient excitement and energy for the issue under discussion. Allow everyone in the audience to sense your presence. Smile naturally, without pushing anything. Flow effortlessly and show everyone how much you appreciate being there.

Remember that public speaking is a talent that develops with practice and experience. Developing good public speaking abilities is critical for both personal and professional success. It dramatically decreases worry and increases confidence, both of which are required for success in practically every part of life. Maybe you don't say much in public, but you never know when you'll need to speak in front of a large crowd. You better be prepared than sorry.

Chapter 4

Expressing Empathy in Communication

Companies are no longer seen by the public as exist just to maximize profits. People hold them in high regard as a brand and consider them to be a member of the community. Workers and clients choose businesses according to their principles and conduct. You're sure to face financial and reputational calamity if you don't pay attention to and address the issues raised by employees who are the backbone of your business. Empathetic communication is one strategy to enhance connections between employers and employees as well as between businesses and customers, all while creating a more compassionate workplace.

In Communication, What is Empathy?

Understanding and understanding another person's emotions is the foundation of empathy in communication. To demonstrate your concern for people as individuals, you must actively listen to your audience, acknowledge their feelings, and answer accordingly.

Empathic communication improves trust, loyalty, and the overall profitability of your small company by helping to establish good connections with both consumers and staff.

For Successful Communication to Occur, Why is Empathy Important?

Ignorant communication may result in fights, snap judgments, and betrayal of confidence. As it relates to business, this might mean:

Sales Lost: Customers may get disenchanted with companies and salespeople who lack empathy or disregard significant civic issues.

Tarnished Reputation: When more staff members and clients see your company's callousness, it may encourage critics to voice their opinions about you.

Staff Turnover: Employee retention is lowered when there is a persistent lack of empathy shown to them.

Reduced Productivity: Long-term performance may suffer if staff members are confronting personal difficulties and are unable to discuss them with management.

According to 59% of workers, speaking with a manager or HR about mental health concerns might jeopardize their job security because 77% of CEOs are concerned that they may become less respected if they show too much empathy.

Nevertheless, they will discover that the time investment is well worth it when they consider the advantages for the business.

A sympathetic business, for instance, may boost employee engagement, according to 70% of workers and HR experts.

Added advantages consist are:

- Enhanced morale among staff members as a result of having supervisors who are attentive to their requirements.
- An improvement in teamwork and mutual regard.
- Enhanced engagement and productivity because employees feel appreciated and supported.

- More devoted customers when they see your business as compassionate (when discussing humanitarian concerns)
- Decreased attrition among employees.

Communication Skills Based on Empathy

Therefore, what abilities are necessary to develop empathy-based communication effectively? Does it provide support for someone to weep on? Is it being too cooperative, perhaps?

To be empathetic, one must comprehend the perspective of the other person; it is not necessary to strive to fix their problems or express pity for them. Put yourself in their position and try to understand why they feel the way they do. This doesn't mean you have to agree with them or feel sorry for them.

There are two more abilities to hone in:

1. A Consciousness of Oneself

Understanding and being able to identify your emotions, ideas, and actions. To comprehend how your activities affect team dynamics and corporate culture, self-awareness might be essential.

Think about how your communication style affects the team, for instance, and give it some thought. Building empathy and better connections may be achieved by acknowledging and addressing issues that need improvement.

2. Intuition for Emotions

the capacity to be aware of, comprehend, and regulate your own emotions as well as those of other people. Effective communication and collaboration may be enhanced by a leader who can perceive their team members' emotions and react accordingly.

How to Engage in Empathetic Communication

A leader must acquire and put empathy into practice via communication. So here are some pointers for consistently talking with empathy:

Display clues without words: Words may not always translate into action. One's empathy is not just based on their words; it also depends on "How" one expresses themselves. You can read someone's true thoughts by their body language.

Make eye contact and sometimes nod in agreement while someone is speaking to demonstrate that you are paying attention.

Another way to show empathy and understanding is via facial expressions, such as a worried or contemplative look.

It takes self-awareness to understand your responses and the reasons behind them before you can enhance your nonverbal clues. To respond with true empathy, you must then learn to reset your emotions and mentality.

Considering as Opposed to.
Explanation: You should never expect to understand someone else's meaning or motivations when they speak. Seek clarification rather than jumping to conclusions to make sure the talk is fruitful. You can guarantee that everyone is on the same page by asking clarifying questions to assist you in comprehending other people's perspectives.

An employee may not be intending to be lazy, for example, if they want to work from home full-time. Question their reasoning for that choice. It might be that they have a health issue that makes driving or controlling symptoms at work difficult, or they may have to care for a young kid and cannot afford daycare.

Open-mindedness against Criticism:
Try to understand things from their perspective rather than discounting the thoughts and opinions of others when they conflict with your own.

Perhaps you believe that remaining at home isn't the best option while having a health issue of your own and coming to work anyhow. However, different people handle personal matters in different ways, and some people choose to keep their affairs private.

"When we judge or criticize someone internally, we tend to create a hostile and tense environment, Instead, go into each conversation with an open mind and be willing to find common ground with the person you're speaking with."

Employing Forceful Words: Expressing your ideas and emotions in a clear, confident, straightforward, and non-aggressive manner without being confrontational or submissive is known as assertive communication. Being truthful without coming off as impolite is empowered by it.

Assertive communication can foster more constructive dialogue and prevent defensiveness or conflict. One way to convey empathy without being judged or criticized is via assertive or nonjudgmental communication.

Show Patience and Attentive Listening Skills: People often find it difficult to listen during arguments before responding. Be patient and let the other person talk to foster more empathic communication. Try to make sure you grasp what they're saying while you're actively listening to them.

When you are thinking about responses and defenses rather than listening to what is being said, become conscious of it. Note it down, then "switch off" your mind so that you can concentrate on the other individual.

Here are some pointers for enhancing attentive hearing:

- Maintain eye contact
- If anything is unclear to you, ask inquiries.

- To make sure you comprehended what was said, paraphrase or summarize it.
- While someone is speaking, refrain from multitasking by not checking your phone or sending an email.

It is possible to validate someone else's feelings without endorsing them.

Brand image and a better workplace may be achieved via the use of empathy in communication. More positive dialogues may result from it, as well as improved relationships based on mutual respect and understanding.

Simply be more receptive to the ideas and emotions of others and have an open mind. You may build trust and make everyone's surroundings more productive by keeping these pointers in mind.

Chapter 5

Creating Emotional Bonds

Making decisions is often influenced by emotions. Research indicates that emotions often take precedence over reason when it comes to decision-making, despite our desire to think that our judgments are entirely rational. When it comes to individuals and businesses that we feel good about, can connect to, and feel like they understand us personally, we are more inclined to buy from them or build enduring relationships with them.

There is more to building emotional relationships than meeting basic needs or offering workable answers. Understanding your clients' individual beliefs, aspirations, and driving forces is necessary. This entails developing a closer relationship with your customers, appreciating their distinct viewpoints, and discovering shared experiences and mutual interests. A feeling of trust and camaraderie that transcends a transactional connection is fostered when you can establish personal communication with your customers.

Making emotional relationships requires understanding and empathy above everything else. Putting yourself in your client's shoes can help you better understand their needs and worries and provide answers that are customized for their unique situation. Customers are more likely to form a deep emotional connection with your business when they see that their needs are being addressed and that you are paying attention to them.

Shared experiences are a crucial component of emotional bonds. People are drawn to those who share their background, hobbies, or experiences inherently. Finding and using these shared experiences with your customers helps you create a feeling of belonging and community, both of which are critical for building enduring connections.

In the end, building rapport and trust with your customers is what emotional connections are all about. Establishing a solid and long-lasting connection begins with your ability to provide pleasant emotional experiences and show that you care about your customers' lives and well-being. We'll look at several methods in the next part for building emotional bonds with your customers.

Building solid and long-lasting relationships with customers requires building deep emotional connections with them. Through fostering an emotional connection, companies may build a feeling of trust and loyalty with their customers that will keep them coming back time and time again.

Developing an Emotional Bond with Your Audience

Know your Audience: Knowing your audience is the first step to connecting with them on an emotional level. You need to understand their identity, priorities, and issues. To learn more about the psychographics, behavior, and demographics of your audience, you may use methods like personas, interviews, surveys, and social media listening. Your ability to adapt your message to your audience's tastes, motives, and pain points will increase with your familiarity with them.

In an Acceptable Tone: Your attitude, personality, and emotions are all expressed in the tone of your conversation. Depending on your brand voice and the expectations of your audience, it might be formal or casual, friendly or professional, comical or serious. Using the right tone with your audience may help you build trust, rapport, and empathy. Use a conversational and lighthearted tone, for instance, if your audience is young and informal. You may speak authoritatively and courteously if your audience is older and conservative.

Storytelling: By appealing to the imagination, curiosity, and emotions of your audience, stories are a powerful way to establish an emotional connection. Telling compelling and memorable tales may help you communicate your brand values, highlight client success stories, and highlight the advantages of your product. Effective tales must have a distinct structure, an intriguing premise, a sympathetic protagonist, a pertinent conflict, and a satisfying conclusion. To bring your story to life, you must also use vivid language, sensory elements, and feelings.

Be Empathetic: The capacity to understand and feel another person's feelings is known as empathy. By exhibiting your concern for their wants, difficulties, and goals, you may establish an emotional connection with your audience. By establishing a feeling of connection and belonging via the use of pronouns like "you," "we," or "us," you may demonstrate empathy. By addressing the problems of your audience, providing answers, or expressing thanks, admiration, or support, you may also show empathy.

Add Value: Provide something useful, relevant, or advantageous to your audience to provide value. By showcasing your knowledge, kindness, and reliability, it might assist you in developing an emotional connection with your audience. By providing useful material, such as guidance, thoughts, resources, or suggestions, you may provide value. Additionally, you may provide value by providing your audience with awards, discounts, or incentives. Your audience is more likely to respond with loyalty, involvement, and advocacy if you provide more value.

Building long-term relationships and fostering loyalty with your audience will be facilitated by your consistent display of empathy, sincerity, genuine concern for their well-being, and deep emotional connections.

www.ingramcontent.com/pod-product-compliance
Lightning Source LLC
Chambersburg PA
CBHW071001290526
45795CB00005B/1732